P9-BZH-175

The
Stamp Act of 1765

by Michael Burgan

Content Adviser: Richard J. Bell,
History Department,
Harvard University

Reading Adviser: Susan Kesselring, M.A., Literacy Educator,
Rosemount-Apple Valley-Eagan (Minnesota) School District

Compass Point Books ◆ Minneapolis, Minnesota

Compass Point Books
151 Good Counsel Drive
P.O. Box 669
Mankato, MN 56002-0669

This book was manufactured with paper containing
at least 10 percent post-consumer waste.

On the cover: In protest of the Stamp Act of 1765, people burn stamps in New York City.

Photographs ©: North Wind Picture Archives, cover, 6, 7, 11, 13, 17, 18, 22, 26, 29, 30, 33, 38; Prints Old &
Rare, back cover (far left); Library of Congress, back cover, 15, 31, 37, 39; Stock Montage, 4, 5, 10, 19, 36,
41; Hulton/Archive by Getty Images, 8, 28; Bettmann/Corbis, 9, 35; Canadian Heritage Gallery/National
Archives of Canada, C-140172, 14; Colonial Williamsburg Foundation, 20; DVIC/NARA, 23; National
Portrait Gallery, Smithsonian Institution/Art Resource, N.Y., 25; National Park Service, artist Louis S.
Glanzman, 27; Mary Evans Picture Library, 34.

Creative Director: Terri Foley
Managing Editor: Catherine Neitge
Editor: Nadia Higgins
Photo Researcher: Svetlana Zhurkina
Designer/Page production: Bradfordesign, Inc./Bobbie Nuytten
Educational Consultant: Diane Smolinski
Cartographer: XNR Productions, Inc.

Library of Congress Cataloging-in-Publication Data
Burgan, Michael.
   The Stamp Act of 1765 / by Michael Burgan.
      p. cm. — (We the people)
   Includes bibliographical references (p.   ) and index.
   ISBN 978-0-7565-0846-3
1. Great Britain. Stamp Act (1765)—Juvenile literature. 2. United States—History—Revolution,
1775–1783—Causes—Juvenile literature. I. Title. II. We the people (Series) (Compass Point Books)
E215.2.B87 2004
973.3'111—dc22   2004016303

Visit Compass Point Books on the Internet at *www.compasspointbooks.com*
or e-mail your request to *custserv@compasspointbooks.com*

TABLE OF CONTENTS

A CHALLENGE TO BRITISH RULE

During the summer of 1765, thousands of Americans stormed out of their homes and into the streets. They were angry with Great Britain. At this time, the United States was not yet a country. Instead, 13 American colonies were ruled by the British government.

Great Britain was demanding that its American colonies pay a new tax on all kinds of papers and documents—even playing cards.

In 1765, Britain's Parliament made laws, such as the Stamp Act, that ruled the American colonies.

4

Americans in Boston react with dismay as they read the Stamp Act.

The law calling for the tax was named the Stamp Act.
Many colonists thought the Stamp Act was unfair, and
they showed their anger in violent protests.

5

The protests in North America worried some British officials. Members of the British Parliament debated what to do. Benjamin Franklin, a famous American political leader, told the British lawmakers that the Stamp Act would cause bad feelings between Great Britain and the colonies. In 1766, Parliament finally decided to repeal the Stamp Act. The Americans would not have to pay the tax after all. However, the British lawmakers claimed they had the right to collect other taxes in the future.

Many Americans disagreed with the British lawmakers. Even though they were under British rule, the Americans did not elect members of Parliament. They had no say about how laws were made. Unlike people living in England,

Colonists protest the Stamp Act at a parade in New York.

6

the Americans had no representatives to vote on the tax laws that would affect their daily lives. Angry Americans said there could be "no taxation without representation."

The colonies became more peaceful after Great Britain repealed the Stamp Act. However, the issue of taxation without representation did not go away. The Stamp Act marked the first serious American challenge to British power. Today, it is viewed as a major step on the path to American independence from Great Britain.

Protests against the Stamp Act sometimes grew out of control.

7

GREAT BRITAIN'S CHANGE IN ATTITUDE

During the first half of the 1700s, Great Britain did not pay much attention to what the colonies did, and the Americans liked it that way. Though the British collected taxes, called duties, on certain goods brought into the colonies, the Americans often avoided the duties by shipping goods illegally. British officials mostly ignored this smuggling.

A trading ship like this one brought goods into the colonies.

In general, British leaders were too concerned with events in Europe to worry about taxes in North America.

The British attitude toward its colonies changed sharply in 1760. That year, George III became king of England. George thought Parliament

King George III of England

had unfairly limited the power of previous kings. He and his advisers took more control of the government. They also began to play a larger role in governing the colonies.

A war with France also focused more British attention on North America. In 1754, colonists fought

9

British troops in battle during the French and Indian War

several times with French forces in western Pennsylvania and Virginia. At the time, France owned large parts of North America and was competing with Great Britain to control this region. The fighting between the Americans and the French led to the French and Indian War. France received help from different American Indian tribes as it battled American and British troops.

10

By 1763, the British had defeated the French. They took over France's lands in eastern Canada. They also won French territory along the western side of the 13 American colonies. These western lands were the home of many Indians who had supported the

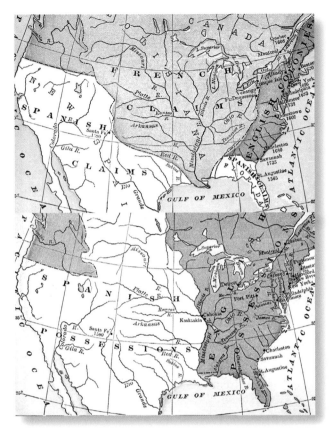

These maps from the 1700s show how land changed hands between France and Great Britain as a result of the French and Indian War.

French. Even before the war, American colonists had been moving into that region, and they sometimes attacked the Indians. Now that Great Britain controlled their homeland, the Native Americans feared even more Americans would come.

For a time, an Indian chief named Pontiac led the tribes in another war against the British. Pontiac and his warriors wanted to stop the colonists' westward movement. To calm the Indians, British officials promised to protect them from the colonists. In October 1763, King George III

This map shows the American colonies and surrounding lands in 1763.

Chief Pontiac

issued an order known as the Royal Proclamation of 1763. It said that the Americans could not settle on lands west of the Allegheny Mountains without British permission. These mountains cut through western Virginia and continue north to Pennsylvania.

The proclamation, however, was not just to protect the Native Americans. Some British officials wanted to keep the colonists near the Atlantic Ocean to increase British trade with the Americans. The British feared that if the colonists moved too far inland, they wouldn't trade as much with British merchants overseas. With seaports too far away, it would be easier for the Americans to make

13

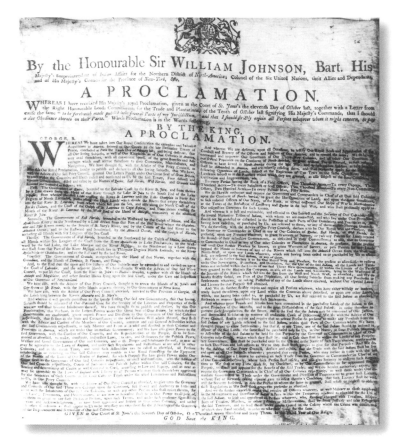

The Royal Proclamation of 1763

their own goods. Also, the Americans might buy from French or Spanish merchants in western parts of North America.

Great Britain did not want any other nation gaining influence over the colonies. Keeping the colonists east of the Allegheny Mountains would make it easier for the British to control them.

FROM THE SUGAR ACT TO THE STAMP ACT

Great Britain sent troops to its new western American lands to make sure the Royal Proclamation was obeyed. The British government needed money to pay for these troops and other expenses in North America. At the time, George Grenville was the prime minister of Great Britain. In that role, he was the most powerful member of Parliament. Grenville thought that the Americans should pay part of the costs for "defending, protecting and securing" the colonies.

George Grenville, prime minister of Great Britain

15

In 1764, Grenville wrote the law that came to be known as the Sugar Act. The law placed new duties on certain goods, such as coffee, lumber, and sugar. At the same time, the Sugar Act reduced an old duty on molasses, which had been in place since 1733. Molasses was important to the colonists because they used it to make rum, which they sold overseas. Before the Sugar Act, merchants avoided the duty on molasses by smuggling it into the colonies.

Grenville hoped the Americans would stop smuggling molasses if the duty were lower. He also planned to send naval ships to catch any remaining smugglers and collect the duty. Anyone caught smuggling would be tried in an admiralty court. The accused smugglers would face a British judge, not an American jury. In the past, local juries had often let accused colonial smugglers go free.

American rum makers quickly protested the Sugar Act. They did not want to pay *any* duty on molasses. They also did want not to be punished for smuggling, since they had done this freely in the past. In North Carolina, the colony's lawmakers argued that the law was unfair. They said the Sugar Act went against the "right … and privilege of imposing our own taxes." In other words, the law was an example of taxation without representation.

Even before the Sugar Act took effect, Grenville was planning another tax. In Great Britain, people had to pay a tax on most printed papers. These included legal papers, business documents, and newspapers. People who created public documents paid a tax on the blank paper they bought. Officials placed a stamp on the blank paper after the tax was paid. Grenville wanted the Americans to pay the same kind of tax, so in February 1765 he asked Parliament to pass a Stamp Act for the colonies.

Stamps such as these showed the tax had been paid. Words on the stamps refer to British money, such as a halfpenny or shilling, that was used in the colonies.

A

TABLE

Of the Prices of Parchment and Paper for the Service

of *America*.

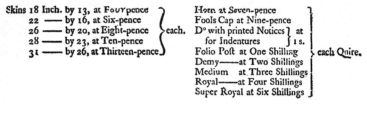

Parchment.

Skins 18 Inch. by 13, at Four-pence
22 —— by 16, at Six-pence
26 —— by 20, at Eight-pence } each.
28 —— by 23, at Ten-pence
31 —— by 26, at Thirteen-pence

Paper.

Horn at Seven-pence
Fools Cap at Nine-pence
D° with printed Notices } at
for Indentures } 1 s.
Folio Post at One Shilling } each Quire.
Demy——at Two Shillings
Medium at Three Shillings
Royal——at Four Shillings
Super Royal at Six Shillings

Paper for Printing

News.

Double Crown at 14 s. } each Ream.
Double Demy at 19 s.

Almanacks.

Book—Crown Paper at 10 s. 6 d.
Book——Fools Cap at 6 s. 6 d. } each Ream.
Pocket — Folio Post at 20 s.
Sheet——Demy at 13 s.

*This chart shows the prices the British government charged for various kinds
and sizes of stamped documents.*

The people most affected by this new tax were

lawyers, merchants, printers, and ministers—some of

the most influential people in society. Also, more people

would have to pay the new tax than those who had to

pay the duty on molasses. The Stamp Act meant that a larger group of Americans would have a higher cost for running their business.

Some Americans in Great Britain told Grenville that the colonies would not accept the tax. A few colonial leaders suggested that Great Britain should let the colonies raise the money needed for troops with their own taxes.

British soldiers guard stamped paper as it is carried to the city hall in New York.

19

Grenville, however, was not only interested in raising money. He wanted to show the colonists that Parliament had a right to tax them.

Parliament passed the Stamp Act in March. The law forced the colonists to pay the tax with silver coins, which were often hard to find in North America. Furthermore, as with the Sugar Act, people accused of disobeying the Stamp Act would be tried by British judges in admiralty courts.

Colonists had to pay for stamps with hard-to-find silver coins such as this one, shown front and back.

ANGRY WORDS ACROSS THE ATLANTIC OCEAN

When they learned about the Stamp Act, many Americans wrote and spoke out against it. Once again, some people complained that they were being taxed unfairly, since they did not have any representatives in Parliament.

A Virginia lawmaker named Patrick Henry wrote that the Americans should have all the "liberties … enjoyed and possessed by the people of Great Britain." Those liberties included paying only the taxes they approved of, through their representatives. If the Americans had representatives in Parliament, they might have convinced other members not to pass the Stamp Act. At the least, the American representatives would be able to influence how the law was written. Without representation, the Americans were stuck with whatever tax law Parliament passed.

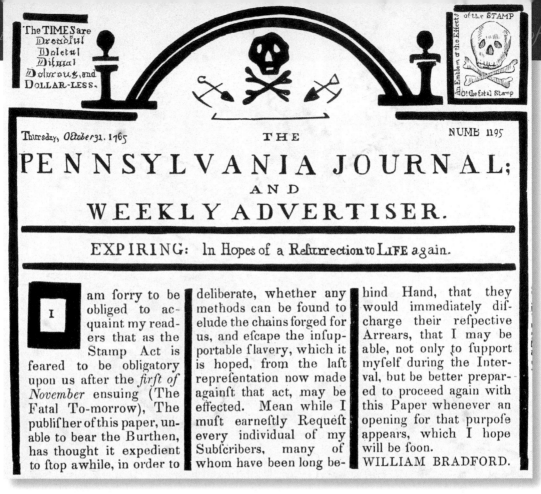

This publication from October 31, 1765, was full of articles such as this one speaking out against the Stamp Act.

Other Americans argued that Parliament did have a right to collect certain taxes called external taxes. A duty was an external tax because it applied to goods that came from outside the colonies. Parliament was responsible for trade between Great Britain and all its colonies across the British Empire, so it could raise external taxes.

Internal taxes, however, were a different story. That kind of tax applied to activities carried out strictly within the colonies. Some Americans claimed that only colonial lawmakers, not British lawmakers, should collect internal taxes. The Stamp Act was an internal tax.

Patrick Henry makes an angry speech against the Stamp Act to fellow lawmakers in Virginia.

23

In Great Britain, some people attacked the arguments against the Stamp Act. They believed the Americans were simply trying to avoid the tax and were not willing to pay for their own protection. One newspaper article noted that British residents were paying higher taxes since the French and Indian War, so how could the colonists "expect that no addition whatsoever will be made to theirs?"

Some British lawmakers disagreed that the Stamp Act was taxation without representation. They said that the colonists had virtual representation. Members of Parliament represented the interests of *all* British citizens—including the colonists. They did not just work on behalf of the small group of people who actually elected them. The lawmakers pointed out that many British residents did not vote for representatives, either. Yet they accepted the taxes Parliament passed. Those residents, like the Americans, had virtual representation. Since the Americans were represented virtually, they should accept the Stamp Act.

PROTESTING THE STAMP ACT

By August 1765, Americans who were against the Stamp Act wanted to do more than just debate it. They believed protests would convince Parliament to repeal the tax. In Boston, a group called the Loyal Nine organized a gang of local men to lead a protest against Andrew Oliver. The British government had named Oliver the stamp commissioner for Massachusetts, which meant he was in charge of collecting the new tax.

On August 14, the protesters hung an effigy of Oliver from a tree. The

Andrew Oliver, stamp commissioner for Massachusetts

An effigy of a stamp commissioner hung by American protesters

effigy looked like Oliver. They later took it down, chopped off its head, and burned it. As many as 5,000 people joined the protest during the day. At one point, an angry mob broke into Oliver's home and threatened to kill him. Later in August, the Boston protesters marched again. This time they targeted Thomas Hutchinson. The lieutenant governor had many political enemies in the city. Some residents linked him with both the Stamp Act and other British policies they opposed. At Hutchinson's house, the mob stole books, clothing, and furniture. Governor Francis Bernard later wrote that "everything movable was destroyed."

An angry mob destroys Thomas Hutchinson's house in Boston.

27

Thomas Hutchinson's wig flies off his head as he runs away from violent protesters in Boston.

Boston's Loyal Nine soon renamed themselves the Sons of Liberty. In other colonies, people who opposed the Stamp Act formed their own Sons of Liberty groups. Some women also opposed the Stamp Act, and they formed the Daughters of Liberty.

From Boston, the protests spread to other cities. Residents of Newport, Rhode Island, attacked the homes of several wealthy men, including the colony's stamp commissioner. In New York City, 2,000 people destroyed the home of a British military officer.

As news of the protests spread, stamp commissioners across the colonies quit their jobs. Other men who were offered the jobs refused to take them. By November, no colony had a commissioner ready to collect the Stamp Act. One American minister wrote to a friend in England,

Paul Revere, who would later become famous for his role in the Revolutionary War, was a member of the Sons of Liberty in Boston. Here, he distributes political notices for the group.

Protesters burn stamped papers in New York.

"I am satisfied [the Stamp Act] will never be carried …
[out], unless it is done at the point of a Sword."

Other protests were more peaceful. Lawmakers in
Massachusetts called for a meeting among the colonies to
discuss the Stamp Act. In October, representatives from nine
colonies met in New York City. This meeting was called the
Stamp Act Congress. After two weeks of debate, the
Stamp Act Congress released a set of 14 statements dealing
with the Stamp Act.

A Pennsylvania newspaper made fun of the Stamp Act by suggesting that this skull and crossbones stamp be put on documents.

The representatives accepted that the colonists had to obey King George III and Parliament, just as the people of Great Britain did. At the same time, they insisted that the Americans should have the same rights as British residents. One of the most important rights was that "no taxes be imposed on them, but with their own Consent, given personally, or by their Representatives." The congress dismissed the idea of virtual representation. Representatives also spoke out against the admiralty courts and said that a trial by jury—not just by a single judge—was a basic British right. In the end, the congress told Parliament and King George that the colonies would try to force a repeal of the Stamp Act.

THE BRITISH RESPOND

News of the American protests worried some British officials. In December 1765, George Grenville wanted Parliament to declare that the Americans were rebels and should be punished. Other lawmakers, however, began to think that the Stamp Act should be repealed. They did not want to risk creating even more problems in the colonies. These lawmakers also had a practical concern—the American response to the tax was hurting trade between the colonies and Great Britain.

When the Sugar Act was passed in 1764, some American merchants stopped buying goods from the British. They hoped that if British merchants and manufacturers lost business, they would force Parliament to repeal the Sugar Act. After the Stamp Act, even more Americans joined this boycott of most British goods. They said they would not buy from the British until Parliament repealed the Stamp Act. The

Sons of Liberty sometimes went so far as to threaten Americans who refused to go along with the boycott.

The American boycott worked. British merchants and manufacturers began to lose money. They worried they would lose even more if Parliament did not repeal the Stamp Act. The merchants did not care much about such issues as taxation without representation or virtual representation. They just wanted to make sure their businesses survived.

In December, merchants and manufacturers from across Great Britain asked Parliament to end the tax. The lawmakers heard that many British

WILLIAM JACKSON,

an *IMPORTER*; at the

BRAZEN HEAD,

North Side of the **TOWN-HOUSE,**

and *Oppofite the Town-Pump, in*

Corn-hill, **BOSTON.**

It is defired that the SONS and DAUGHTERS of *LIBERTY,* would not buy any one thing of him, for in fo doing they will bring Difgrace upon *themfelves*, and their *Pofterity,* for *ever* and *ever*, AMEN

The Sons of Liberty distributed flyers such as this one to support their boycott. This notice tells people not to buy goods from William Jackson, who continued to trade with the British in spite of the boycott.

33

During the Stamp Act boycott, British merchants lost trade with the colonies.

workers had already lost their jobs, and thousands more would be out of work if the boycott continued. Some leaders feared that the people who lost their jobs might start their own protests, just as the Americans had done.

34

In January 1766, Parliament began debating what to do about the Stamp Act. Some lawmakers argued the law had to be continued. They insisted the Americans did not have a legal right to resist the tax. These lawmakers feared that if they gave in on this tax, the colonists would protest future taxes or any British efforts to control them. To prevent more protests, Parliament had to show its power.

Other lawmakers favored repeal. William Pitt, a famous British lawmaker, told Parliament, "I rejoice that America has resisted." He said the British did have the right to pass laws that affected the colonists. However, Parliament could not tax the Americans without their consent. Many Americans had been saying

British lawmaker William Pitt

35

the same thing since Parliament first passed the Stamp Act.

In February, Benjamin Franklin spoke in Parliament. He said that before 1763, Americans had "not only a respect, but an affection, for Great Britain [and] for its laws, its custom and manners." The

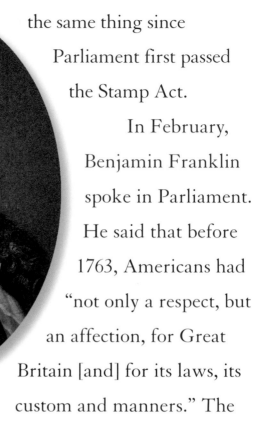

Benjamin Franklin

Sugar and Stamp Acts had destroyed those good feelings. Now, Franklin said, the Americans would never accept the Stamp Act. They believed Parliament did not have the legal power to collect an internal tax and that the lawmakers were weakening their rights.

GOOD NEWS—AND BAD

Franklin's words and the British merchants' efforts had a strong effect. A week after Franklin spoke, Parliament voted to repeal the Stamp Act. Across London, people celebrated. They knew the American boycott of British goods would end. British merchants and manufacturers would begin hiring again. Since there was no radio or television at the time, the Americans did not hear the news

A British political cartoon celebrates the Stamp Act's "funeral."

37

until several weeks later. When they did, many Americans filled the streets and praised both William Pitt and King George.

Some Americans believed their protests were what had convinced the British to repeal the Stamp Act. Some thought Parliament had accepted their arguments about taxation without representation.

The colonists soon learned, however, that while Parliament had changed its policies,

Glorious News.

BOSTON, Friday 11 o'Clock, 16th *May* 1766.

THIS Instant arrived here the Brig Harrison, belonging to *John Hancock*, Esq; Captain *Shubael Coffin*, in 6 Weeks and 2 Days from LONDON, with important News, as follows.

From the LONDON GAZETTE.

Westminster, March 18th, 1766.

THIS day his Majesty came to the House of Peers, and being in his royal robes seated on the throne with the usual solemnity, Sir Francis Moli- neux, Gentleman Usher of the Black Rod, was sent with a Message from his Majesty to the House of Commons, commanding their atten- dance in the House of Peers. The Commons being come thither accordingly, his Majesty was pleased to give his royal assent to

An ACT to REPEAL an Act made in the last Session of Parliament, in- tituled, an Act for granting and applying certain Stamp-Duties and other Duties in the British Colonies and Plantations in America, towards further defraying the expences of defending, protecting and securing the same, and for amending such parts of the several Acts of Parliament relating to the trade and revenues of the said Colonies and Plantations, as direct the manner of determining and recovering the penalties and forfeitures therein mentioned.

Also ten public bills, and seventeen private ones.

Yesterday there was a meeting of the principal Merchants concerned in the American trade, at the King's Arms tavern in Cornhill, to consider of an Ad- dress to his Majesty on the beneficial Repeal of the late Stamp-Act.

Yesterday morning about eleven o'clock a great number of North American Merchants went in their coaches from the King's Arms tavern in Cornhill to the House of Peers, to pay their duty to his Majesty, and to express their satisfac- tion at his signing the Bill for Repealing the American Stamp-Act, there was upwards of fifty coaches in the procession.

Last night the said gentlemen dispatched an express for Falmouth, with fif- teen copies of the Act for repealing the Stamp-Act, to be forwarded immediate- ly for New York.

Orders are given for several merchantmen in the river, to proceed to sea im- mediately on their respective voyages to North America, some of whom have been cleared out since the first of November last.

Yesterday messengers were dispatched to Birmingham, Sheffield, Manchester, and all the great manufacturing towns in England, with an account of the final decision of an august assembly relating to the Stamp-Act.

When the KING went to the House of Peers to give the Royal Assent, there was such a vast Concourse of People, huzzaing, clapping Hands, &c. that it was several Hours before His Majesty reached the House.

Immediately on His Majesty's Signing the Royal Assent to the Repeal of the Stamp-Act, the Merchants trading to America dispatched a Vessel which had been in waiting, to put into the first Port on the Continent with the Account.

There were the greatest Rejoicings possible in the City of London, by all Ranks of People, on the TOTAL Repeal of the Stamp-Act.—The Ships in the River displayed all their Colours, Illuminations and Bonfires in many Parts. — In short, the Rejoicings were as great as were ever known on any Occasion.

It is said the Acts of Trade relating to America would be taken under Con- sideration, and all Grievances removed. The Friends to America are very pow- erful, and disposed to assist us to the utmost of their Ability.

Capt. Blake sailed the same Day with Capt. Coffin, and Capt. Shand a Fort- night before him, both bound to this Port.

It is impossible to express the Joy the Town is now in, on receiving the above, great, glorious and important NEWS—The Bells in all the Churches were immediately set a Ringing, and we hear the Day for a general Rejoicing will be the beginning of next Week.

PRINTED for the Benefit of the PUBLIC, by *Drapers, Edes & Gill, Green & Russell,* and *Fleets.* The Customers to the Boston Papers may have the above gratis at their respective Offices.

[Fac-simile of an original in the library of the Mass. Hist. Society. — ED.]

A flyer announces the repeal of the Stamp Act in Boston.

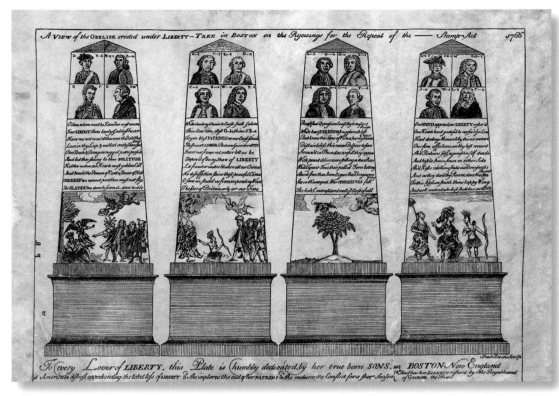

This illustration shows all four sides of a Boston monument that celebrates the end of the Stamp Act. The dedication at the bottom reads, "To every Lover of liberty, this Plate is humbly dedicated, by her true born Sons, in Boston New England."

it had not changed its thinking. As it repealed the Stamp Act, Parliament passed a new law. This Declaratory Act stated that Parliament had the "full power and authority to make laws … to bind the colonies and people of America, subjects of the crown of Great Britain, in all cases whatsoever." In the future, Parliament said, it would ignore any American arguments for limiting Great Britain's right to govern the colonies as it chose.

Americans disagreed about what the Declaratory Act meant. Some said it applied to both internal and external taxes. Others believed Parliament did not plan to put new taxes on the colonies. These people thought Parliament accepted what the Americans and Pitt had argued before—that the British could pass laws affecting the Americans, but they could not tax the colonists without their consent.

The Declaratory Act did not end the debate between the Americans and the British over taxes. In 1767, Parliament passed new duties on many goods. The British assumed the Americans would accept them, since they were external taxes. Now, however, many Americans were opposed to *any* tax without their consent.

The issues first raised by the Stamp Act continued to create disagreements between Great Britain and its colonies. These disagreements led to new efforts by Parliament to control the colonies. By 1775, the Americans were ready to fight for their rights, and so the American Revolutionary War began. Within eight years, the Americans won their independence from Great Britain.

After the Stamp Act, Americans became even bolder about fighting British taxes. Here, a colonial woman chases off a British tax collector with a broom.

GLOSSARY

admiralty court—court that addresses legal issues involving ships and sailors

boycott—refusal to buy certain goods as a form of protest

commissioner—a person chosen for a certain government job

duty—a tax charged on goods coming from outside a country

external—happening outside a country

internal—happening within a country

lieutenant governor—a state government official who is second in command after the governor

Parliament—the part of the British government that makes laws

repeal—to overturn a law

representatives—people chosen to support the interests of a larger group

virtual—almost or as good as real

DID YOU KNOW?

- After 1765, Americans who protested British policies often met under large trees nicknamed Liberty Trees. The last surviving Liberty Tree was in Annapolis, Maryland. A 1999 hurricane damaged the tree, and it had to be cut down.

- The Sons of Liberty sometimes resorted to torture. In the years leading up to the Revolutionary War, the Sons tarred and feathered some colonial officials. For this punishment, a person was coated with boiling hot tar and then covered with feathers.

- In Philadelphia, some people mistakenly thought Benjamin Franklin had supported the Stamp Act while he was in London. This alarmed Franklin's wife, who feared angry protesters would attack the Franklin home. In a letter to her husband, she wrote that she had asked her relatives to bring guns to defend their home. The house, however, was never attacked.

- While fighting Pontiac and his Native American allies, the British sent the Indians some blankets as a gift. The blankets were not a gift at all, however, but a secret weapon. The blankets had actually been infected with smallpox, a deadly disease. Many Indians died from this early example of germ warfare.

IMPORTANT DATES

Timeline

1760	George III becomes the king of Great Britain.
1763	The British win the French and Indian War; King George issues the Royal Proclamation, which forbids Americans from settling west of the Allegheny Mountains.
1764	Parliament approves the Sugar Act.
1765	In March, Parliament passes the Stamp Act; protests against the Stamp Act break out in August; nine colonies send representatives to the Stamp Act Congress in October.
1766	Parliament repeals the Stamp Act but passes the Declaratory Act, which says the British government has the right to pass future taxes.

44

IMPORTANT PEOPLE

KING GEORGE III (1738-1820)
King who tried to strengthen British control over the American colonies

BENJAMIN FRANKLIN (1706-1790)
Politician and inventor who represented the colonies in London and spoke out against the Stamp Act

GEORGE GRENVILLE (1712-1770)
British prime minister who asked Parliament to pass the Stamp Act

THOMAS HUTCHINSON (1711-1780)
Lieutenant governor of Massachusetts whose house was destroyed by Boston residents opposed to the Stamp Act

WILLIAM PITT (1708-1788)
Member of Parliament who supported repeal of the Stamp Act

PONTIAC (1720?-1769)
Native American chief who led a brief war against American settlers and the British

WANT TO KNOW MORE?

More Books to Read

Bohannon, Lisa Frederiksen. *The American Revolution.* Minneapolis: Lerner
   Publications, 2004.

Burgan, Michael. *Colonial and Revolutionary Times.* New York: Franklin
   Watts, 2003.

Gaines, Ann Graham. *King George III: English Monarch.* Philadelphia:
   Chelsea House Publishers, 2001.

Santella, Andrew. *The French and Indian War.* Minneapolis: Compass Point
   Books, 2004.

On the Web

For more information on this topic, use FactHound.

1. Go to *www.facthound.com*

2. Type in this book ID: 0756508460

3. Click on the *Fetch It* button.

FactHound will find the best Web sites for you.

On the Road

The Freedom Trail

The trail's starting point is at:

15 State St.

Boston, MA

For more information about the trail, contact:

The Freedom Trail Foundation

99 Chauncy St.

Boston, MA 02111

617/357-8300

To visit some of the sites where Boston residents led the call for American independence

Look for more We the People books about this era:

African-Americans in the Colonies

The California Missions

The French and Indian War

The Jamestown Colony

The Mayflower Compact

The Plymouth Colony

The Salem Witch Trials

The Thirteen Colonies

Williamsburg

A complete list of We the People titles is available on our Web site:
www.compasspointbooks.com

INDEX

About the Author

Michael Burgan is a freelance writer of books for children and adults. A history graduate from the University of Connecticut, he has written more than 60 fiction and nonfiction children's books for various publishers. For adult audiences, he has written news articles, essays, and plays. Michael Burgan is a recipient of an Edpress Award and belongs to the Society of Children's Book Writers and Illustrators.

DATE DUE

DEMCO 128-5046